A Mother's Guide to

WAKING UP IN AMERICA

LANE KELLER

Published in the United States by Brooklyn Indie Press

www.laneexplains.com

Cover and book design by Chelsea Jewell

Name: Keller, Lane, author.
Title: A Mother's Guide to Waking Up in America
Previously Titled and Printed as : A Mother's New World Order (NWO) Handbook: How to Survive the Illuminati and Other Dangers
Description: First trade paperback original edition. | New York : Brooklyn Indie Press, 2018
Identifiers: ISBN-13: 978-1-941117-06-4

Subjects: BISAC: NONFICTION / Self-help /General. | NONFICTION / Philosophy / Political.

MANUFACTURED IN THE UNITED STATES OF AMERICA

A note to all Citizen-Patriots out there

…Citizen-patriots, from the just beginning to bud, to the stalwart guardians who line their vernacular with phrases like "Give me liberty or give me death," "Do onto others…" or "Where we go one we go all," citizen-patriots are truth-seekers and truthtellers, and to whom Donald Trump, despite his brusque talk and apparent lack of savoir faire, may be nothing less than a modern day Spartacus here to free the slaves from the hold of the lie-infested globalists.

In France people are rising in a populist movement that is beginning to sweep Europe, where the yellow-vested spirit of revolution has come alive in those that see through the plan to dissect, demoralize and annihilate Europe.

In America the phenomenon known as Q-Anon is inciting a mass factfinding quest amongst those with ears to hear, while incurring sneers from the indoctrinated and unaware. Whether by individual or committee, the Q movement threatens to awaken an ever-widening group of individuals whose fealty is to the constitution and not to those who seek to divide, disempower and destroy.

Citizen-patriots are holding the light, pushing the way forward, some having done this for a very for a long time, impatiently at times, occasionally ragged, sometimes dismayed at waiting seemingly-endlessly for the truth to emerge and for the earth to right itself. These individuals are holding space while staying true in their hearts to the cause of a transparent republic where sovereignty reigns, where happiness truly is the right of every being, where the planet is freed from assault, where the air and water is clean, and where all are liberated from the debt slavery which keeps us bent to the grindstone instead of turned toward the stars in innate communion with the divine.

Our sacred right to liberty, transparency from those chosen to represent us, and the union of all humanity—for left to our own devices it is not in our nature to separate, but to cleave, to love, and to unify—is about to manifest, and if not here already, that day will surely be here soon.

— The Author, Dec. 18, 2018

INTRODUCTION

The reasons for writing this small book are varied. I'd just come off of a weekend with my kids. My daughter had just graduated from a southern university and one side of the family being in the north, I'd rented a small beach house within driving distance of all parties. The weekend transpired, as these things go, with fun, laughter and the usual family disagreements.

My partner tended to be emphatic in his opinions and being that his viewpoint differed from everyone else's, his ideas served as a point of contention, particularly with my daughter who, maybe due to her newly-Southern acclimation, sided against each and every point that he made.

An argument ensued wherein she ended up leaving the room crying about how she wanted to live her life in happiness, not dwelling on the bad things that may be going on around us. Her boyfriend, either out of politeness or curiosity, stuck around, and we talked to him about some of the things that are transpiring in the world of which he might have been unaware.

It's very hard for the people of today to comprehend these things unless they've undertaken quite a bit of study along this avenue or grown up in this milieu. The workings of the world are not what we have been taught, and to understand things as they truly are goes against everything we've spent our lives believing. That said, not everyone who's in a position of governing is good or honest, and like it or not, they are part of a system of control that utilizes tactics that are destructive to humanity. These methods as well as the goals behind them, are evil. I can't say it more directly than that.

Most people who are in the government are compromised. They may be good; they may be bad. I'll leave that for other minds to determine. The purpose of this writing is to provide a guideline for the youths and adults of today, and for my own children if they have the inclination. This book should be considered a motherly, loving source that can serve as a jumping off point to further investigation and learning.

The following pages offer a discussion on personal health, love and relationships, religion, the state of politics, and what to do about the different agendas. The purpose of this book is not to frighten. It is to equip.

Like I told my daughter the day following our argument, knowledge will erase fear. Knowledge gives you the tools to fight. Maybe it's best not use the word fight, because the term is frightening to most people. But knowing the truth provides us with the ability to survive, and more than survive, to thrive in this rapidly changing and incredibly challenging world.

1

I grew up in a holistic family. When I was young, let's just say that the go-to lunch box items were baloney on white bread and sometimes, if you were lucky, Skippy peanut butter and some Welch's grape jelly. My family mostly ate green things, which was incredibly progressive for that moment in time, and served as a point of ridicule for my classmates. Undoubtedly, that's where I learned to be strong and to understand that being different wasn't such a terrible thing.

I grew up hearing about the teachings of Adele Davis, who was one of the forerunners of the organic movement, while my own grandfather homesteaded on Long Island before there were communities out there, tending a thriving organic farm that he used to feed his family, the neighbors, nuns from the local convent, and anyone else who came by.

He didn't make money from any of this. The man lived by his wits and knowledge. He was an inventor of sorts who rigged up his own solar panels and an endless variety of farming equipment. One of the things that fascinated me as a child was a stringless tennis racket he used to bat insects off the fruit and vegetables. He would never, ever, use a pesticide.

He grew up in Manitoba, Canada, where I've learned that farming was indeed their way of life, and I can only imagine that our ancestors there would also have never have dreamt of using a pesticide.

I would spend summers on Grandpa's farm, not every summer, not every day but every once in a while. He would point out vegetables and explain how to grow them. There were some tough financial times experienced by my family. My father was in an industry that was hit hard by the recession several times over, and many times we found ourselves the recipients of Grandpa's help.

We would go over there and pick bags and bags of little tomatoes. My mom would turn these into delicious soups and sauces. The most amazing thing were grandpa's zucchini squashes. The zucchini were no less than 5 inches in diameter and they were delicious. It's hard to imagine this, but they were a good 20 inches or more in length. Now, you may say that this is impossible. Did you ever see Woody Allen's movie, "Sleeper?" I kid you not, Grandpa's vegetables were like that. One zucchini mixed with pasta fed us for a week.

I'd like to tell you a little a hint, a little truth that Grandpa shared with me. He said he used to "scavenge" in the neighborhood. At one time there were horses and cows in the streets, or at least there were before my youth, and that's where he got the droppings that he used to fertilize the garden. Sometime after that I supposed he moved on to the more conventional ways of buying cow manure in a bag, or maybe he used droppings from local dogs. No one really knows for sure, but his produce was awe-inspiring.

Of course, Grandpa generated his own seeds year after year. He perfected his own garlic, his own butternut squash, corn, asparagus, tomatoes and much more. Everything was hand sown, raised, and harvested by him, and it was quite a large farm for a man that maintained it all by himself with only an odd helper here and there. So this was a little tiny bit of my upbringing. You can imagine my pain and outrage over how Monsanto and it's paid government lackeys have nearly eradicated organic farming across the globe. Mass suicides of farmers in India, strong-arming small and large countries the world over to use Monsanto's GMO, pesticide-ridden, non self-propagating seeds, have resulted in yielding toxic crops which contain barely 20% of their true nutritional value.

As for my own health, I had the good fortune to have parents who were enlightened and who knew that adulterated food was harmful to the body.

All my friends, well, let's call them not friends, but classmates who ostracized me over this, had their baloney on white bread or Wonderbread, which was enriched flour that forms a ball in your stomach and makes you fat. While they had those things I had stone-ground bread, sprouts, dark green leafy lettuce and some kind of meat or God-knows-what that my mother found at the health food store. My parents were pushing the poverty level at that time, so we ate whatever they could get at the health food store, of which there was only one of on all of Long Island, in Huntington.

My mom used to get quite a bit of her nutritional help from Pearl, who ran that store. I hated going there because I'd end up sitting on the floor for hours where my mom got enlightened on things like whole proteins, because of course there were few books available, other than Adele Davis and a couple of other writers. How do you feed a family when you don't have money to spend on natural foods? You need a mom who is a wizard at making something from nothing, which I was blessed to have.

We did go through an unmentionable vegetarian phase, when there were no vegetarian products to be had, and my mom ended up boiling soy beans that she attempted to pass off as turkeys and other items. This did not go very far with us. If you have ever tasted these little pustules they pretty much came down to eating boils, or toe fungus or something really revolting. We were young and because we did not stand for this, we eventually went back to meat. Other than that, I would say my mom is a miracle worker.

That being said, when my own children were born, I was on a mission to keep them as healthy as possible. The reasons for these were manifold. The world was changing. Multiple vaccinations were prevalent. I learned that vaccines were not effective, that the disease die-off charts were altered, that they contained lethal toxins, and were not tested properly. There were also no long range tests being done, not to mention that the existing test data was skewed. I can provide many links and information on this if you choose to go further, but suffice to say at that time I felt through deep research and soul searching that the best way to go was to not vaccinate my children. At this juncture I hold that conviction tenfold. Vaccines have grown to be far worse, and far more dangerous.

Being a young mother, and quite concerned that I was now leaving my children open to the possibility of illness and other dire things doctors like to scare you with, like diphtheria, whooping cough, polio… I undertook a search to find out how to best keep my children healthy. If we were not going to vaccinate them, and this took quite a lot of convincing on my part since my husband was not at all on the same page, how were we to equip them to fight off diseases?

The answer was actually quite simple and it goes back to my grandfather's farm. You want to make sure their immune system is not compromised in any way. This is still the best way to fight off disease to this day. This is the best advice anyone can give you in terms of your own personal health. Now, what are the main stressors? What are the main things that compromise an immune system?

You're not going to like this unless you've already been open to this way of thinking but here is number one: medicines. Medicines of all types create more problems. There is no medicine, and I'm talking all pharmaceuticals, those that are bought over the counter as well as those prescribed by your doctor, that does not have a side effect. It's a simple truth. Now, some of you are saying, "Well, there are reasons to take to them and there are some occasions…" and I'll leave that open for you decide.

The fact is, medicine does not cure disease. It never has. It never will, and only creates worse problems that need additional treatment, because the trillion dollar pharmaceutical/health care industry will never cut off their money supply by curing you. Oh, yes we're treading on politics here, which we'll get into later but as you'll see if you don't already, the world runs on money. America is not the pillar of virtue we believe our forefathers bequeathed us, despite so many having given up their lives to that end. As far as medicine, I know many of you are saying that you know this or that person was cured by chemotherapy, etc. Chances are that if the patient survived chemotherapy they were young and healthy before the cancer stuck. The die-off rate is immense, especially after the cancer comes back, which it does, all too often. It is a well known fact that a cure for cancer exists and has for many years. Look up the numerous people who have beaten the disease by changing their lifestyles to eliminate stress and going all raw. That is one way. Many cures exist. Many cures for every disease exists. Unfortunately, most of these cures are found within the indigenous cultures that are slowly being eliminated from the planet. The knowledge is still out there if you look for it hard enough. In every situation you need to be discerning and to use your own best inner guidance. Charlatans abound in all areas.

For now, we need to know how to protect ourselves from disease, especially our young children whom we decide not to vaccinate, or whom we do vaccinate.

Pharmaceuticals are one of the main stressors that compromise our immune system. The next would be adulterated food and by that I mean processed food, food that is not in its whole, organic state. "Organic" gets us into another issue because what is labeled organic in the stores is not organic. The FDA, again we're turning on politics here, the FDA in its infinite wisdom and of course at the time the head of the FDA was a former pharmaceutical CEO, pulled a fast one, because Wal-Mart was a heavy lobbyist and still is, and they along with the other chain retailers across the country wanted to put organic food on their shelves. But organic is expensive and their consumer base wouldn't buy expensive products, a fact that's been shown time and again in market research. So, what to do? They lobby the FDA to relax the organic food standards.

This way, they could have something that is slightly organic, slap the label on it, and pass it off as real, allowing the rest of us to feel better about the sugar and additive-laden "organic" cereal they're passing off in Target as being good for our children. It's not the truth. When it comes to organic food what we want is the whole organic product that was in my grandfather's garden. How do we get that, when acquiring it is becoming increasingly difficult, and when the government machinery has all but eradicated our ability to obtain true organic food? If you watched the movie *Food, Inc.* then you've got a pretty good idea of what's going on. But the problem remains, how do we get organic food into our diet? If you don't grow it yourself, with filtered, purified water, with no fertilizers and no pesticides, where do you get it?

You're going to have to find a local farm and you will have to check into them as to what they truly use in their farming practices. Natural is not organic. Then you get together with your neighbors and form a buying co-op, which sounds difficult but once it's done, is quite easy. You can look into organic food co-ops online. If there isn't one where you live then you can form one or create a neighborhood garden where people have equal shares. If this doesn't work, look into hydroponic vertical gardening. This method allows you to grow the largest amount of food possible in the smallest square footage, in your basement or garage with some fluorescent lights, all year round. A step up from hydroponics is aquaponics, which is adding fish and creating your own self-sustaining ecosystem. This will supply you and your family with a continuous supply of non-adulterated produce and protein. You can stay alive and healthy this way with very little cost. Incidentally, you will need organic heirloom seeds and a source of filtered water. For the former, find a seed distributer that has been in business for many years and is not one of the companies cropping up everywhere and capitalizing on people's fears. For filtered water, reverse osmosis remains the most trusted method.

Continuing on the subject of water, it is advisable to get your water tested and to obtain the particular filters you may need to eliminate or reduce the harmful substances it may contain. If you live on or near shale formations, which includes about 75% of the country, make sure to test for hazardous fracking chemicals such as benzene, lead, mercury and strontium, to name a few. If you live in a city you have it easier because regular water analysis tests are mandatory, and posted online. For those of you still in the dark about fluoride, it is not at all necessary to keep your teeth cavity free. Quite the contrary, it is a fraud perpetrated on the public to keep us stupefied, controllable and disconnected from our spiritual selves. Look up fluoride and it's effect on the pineal gland. Studies have shown that remote villages that have never had their water fluoridated have the best teeth. You'll need to look this up. My job is not to prove everything, but to bring it to your awareness. Fluoride is a toxic waste product known to cause, among other things: dementia, severe retardation, lowered IQ, cancerous tumors, muscle disorders, ADD, ADHD, and on and on. Get a filter that is proven effective in reducing fluoride by at least 99%. Nothing else will do.

To put a finer point on processed foods, we've also got to be diligent about allergen/toxins such as refined sugars, wheat, and dairy. The body can grow weak fighting these things off day after day, leaving it too taxed to fight disease. With regard to sugars, unprocessed raw honey that is never heated is a good way to go. Organic stevia is another excellent product. I cooked with it for years and my kids never knew I wasn't using sugar. Notice I did not say "Truvia," which is a synthetic product that is being passed of as Stevia. It should go without saying that your children should never have artificial sweeteners, or sodas of any kind. Sodas contain phosphates among other poisons, and leach calcium from bones. Agave, which is so popular lately, is laden with high fructose corn syrup, although the labels do not say so. You need to call the manufacturers in order to check on this. High fructose corn sugar is an extremely toxic allergen that should not be consumed by anyone, least of all children.

Back to the stressors that compromise our immune system, we've got vaccines, a topic which deserves its own book, but lacking the time and resources to go into that now, it is vital to understand that these are harmful, lethal substances that do not create immunity but instead create lifelong problems, illness, and death. This is an enormous topic and research has already been done by a great many people. Try Vaccine Liberation .org, as a place to start. Understand that contrary to popular belief, it is within our legal right to refuse to vaccinate our children. At the time of this writing every state but two allows a religious exemption. This involves signing a simple form that vaccinating your child goes against your religious beliefs, and filing this form with your school administrator. This same form can follow them to college.

What's next? Environmental toxins, which we are now being besieged with. We have mercury, cadmium, lead, barium, fluoride, strontium and a full array of other lethal toxins coming in from practices like fluoridated water, fracking, and chemtrails, which involve toxins being deliberately sprayed into our environment. You might think that chemtrails, and some of these other things, are in the order of conspiracy theory. To the contrary, they are intentional, and they are real. Chemtrails are extremely common and most of us don't even recognize the white plumes being sprayed over our heads every single day. Almost all cases of Epstein Barr, now Morgellens, even Lyme (Barillia) and also AIDS are being spread by the use of toxins and nano-technology on the air, in our water, and in our food. Yes, you heard right. Lyme is not transferred solely by ticks, and AIDS is not transferred solely by intimate contact. There is a growing list of chronic illnesses being caused by these deliberately disseminated toxins and many of these are contained in the chemtrails that are raining down on us in increasing amounts. Chemtrails are NOT contrails, which are released by jets. Do your research on this.

Going forward, emotional stress is another of the immune killers. Now, we're all going to experience stress and there's meditation and yoga to alleviate it. A quick search on the internet will bring up the process of meditation and yoga breaths for anxiety relief. I have not mastered this in my life. It's an ongoing challenge. What is easier to master, and what is being forced on us in an unnatural manner, is fear-based stress. Fear is not a natural condition. It is being manipulated by the forces controlling us, for one, through the use of a fraudulent monetary, and money-lending system. Charging interest on money is intrinsically wrong. Jesus knew this, as did Lincoln, and JFK. What do those three have in common besides being executed? Jesus railed against the moneylenders. Lincoln was about to abolish the Federal Reserve when he was murdered. JFK had discovered the existence of the NWO and CIA-based deception that caused him to be killed. I can not say for certain that Kennedy was going to change the money system but he knew well enough of it's evils, and he had stated his intention to change things before being assassinated. You can go on believing Lincoln was killed by a man who was angry about him freeing the slaves, or you can learn the truth. We are treading on unpopular politics now, but suffice to say that the killers who have been blamed for these assassinations, as well as those committed throughout history, have merely been front men. There is a far more lethal and insidious force behind each and every one of them.

I cannot pretend to have all the answers regarding these things, but be aware that fear is unnecessary and being deliberately culti-vated. If not eradicated fear will end up imprisoning and killing you. The opposite of fear is love. Send every difficult situation that arises in your life love. Love makes fear go away.

Unconditional love is the answer to everything.

2

I want to point out some resources for protection. There was a machine invented by Wilhelm Reich in the 1950's, an inventor and thinker who was arrested and tortured, and died in jail. Reich was opposed for his way of thinking, and like so many who have had their discoveries suppressed, he was incredibly advanced for his time.

Scientists who have reopened Reich's work have found that he had uncovered a way of altering harmful energies like EMF's, or electromagnetic waves, which are headed our way everyday through cell towers, smart phones, electronic devices and so on. Reich had the foresight to be aware of these things in the 1950's and came up with a way of not only deflecting these waves, but diffusing and transforming them into something positive.

The way to do this is through orgonite, a substance that everyone can make. It's very simple. It's made with both an organic and an inorganic compound. I will point you the resources to follow through on it. If you have to buy it ready made, you can. But there's a big part of orgonite that doesn't necessary got mentioned in many of the sites that sell it. That is the intent of the individual making it.

Those who are aware of the spiritual nature things know of the primary importance of our thoughts. Thought shapes our reality. When creating orgonite intent is very important. Intent is transfused into the material. That's why it is better to make your own. It's not too terribly expensive to make, or too difficult. It's just a little messy.

You need an outer area or at least some place protected by a sheet and you have to be able to open windows for a long while. I will follow with simple instructions and then some links if you want to go further.

There are two other points that the issue of fear brings to mind. Number one is, don't follow the company line. If there's one rule of thumb you carry with you besides loving everyone and everything around you unconditionally, it is: never follow the official response to anything. *Question everything*, and in particular all doctrine, established schools of thought, and whenever some authority figure tells you that something is factual. Look into it, because chances are it is untrue.

Question everything. Look further; look deeply. Use your higher consciousness to find answers and attain the truth. Do not be influenced by the popular line of thought. If there's one rule besides unconditional love that I can leave you with, it would be to question everything, especially those things everyone insists is true. When someone is being ridiculed, or dies unexpectedly, or is in some way outed by the media or by some authority figure, this is always a clue to look deeper. Things are rarely what they seem. Following this line of thought, look at the people who have been discredited over the centuries, turn it around, and find the truth. When a public figure suddenly contracts a deadly disease, dies in a plane crash or car accident, or is killed by a drug overdose, look closer. Find out what really happened in that situation. You'll soon learn that many, many of these individuals were deliberately shut down because they were doing something very important at the time of their deaths They were taken down by a deliberate discrediting, jail, or murder. There is very rarely such a thing as a coincidence.

When the people who run our society encounter somebody who is in their way, there are many different means of getting rid of them. One of these ways is through ridicule, another is through destroying the reputation through criminal charges, mockery or bad press. They can easily create accidents, and disease.

Back to the subject of protection. Orgonite is one means of protecting yourself from environmental toxins. Another item that can help with this is bentonite clay. Bentonite clay is a naturally occurring harmless material that has the ability to absorb toxins, carry them through your body and eliminate them through your urine or excrement. These toxins include lead, and many other heavy metals.

Another helpful substance is zeolite. I can only tell you what my research has been, and I don't claim to have the ultimate answer. I can point you to sources, but the fact is that many people capitalize on the craze of the moment, and zeolite is fast becoming popular as a miracle cure. This is enough for me to doubt popular products, and to go back and try to find the purest from of zeolite available. Whenever a report is released that shows some substance is helpful everyone gets on the internet, publishes reams of testimonials, and tries to make bucks off of it.

Just because some companies make wild claims does not mean you should be discouraged. You need to research what the best proper form of the substance is. I will point you to my sources and what I use.

In general, we're talking about making your body as healthy as possible. There are lots of companies who sell inadequate supplements that can actually harm you. I do think supplements are incredibly important. I'm talking about vitamins and minerals. I think they are extremely critical to our health and well being. My problem is that many of them that say natural are not natural, because they are using artificial processes. It's like those little baby carrots that kids across the country eat. They are dipped in a chlorine bath, which creates a white coating. Chlorine is a known carcinogen.

I believe that whole food supplements are the best, but they are extremely expensive. They are a food and not an extract. Here's another rule of thumb: when the USDA says a certain percentage is what you should take, you can rest assured that it's only in a portion of what you truly need. Vitamin C for maintenance is 1000-3,000 units a day. Vitamin D, which some of us are deprived of due to lack of exposure to the sun, can halt many illnesses. Maintenance is probably between 1,000 or 4,000 units a day depending on what your need is.

When figuring out what you need, there is lab testing, or you can find a highly expert kinesiology practitioner. Our Vitamin D deficiency is part of another scam. We need the sun to survive, at least 20 minutes everyday out in the sun with no sunscreen. Now, sunscreen itself contains a highly toxic chemical named oxybenzone, which creates cancer. The newer sunscreens made with titanium dioxide or zinc oxide are using Nano particles which, because of their size, become toxic, and are linked to genetic changes, Alzheimer's, autism and epilepsy.

Why use sunscreen at all? Have you ever questioned it? Covering up when in the sun longer than twenty minutes, would be the safest way to go. Maybe you only need sunscreen a couple of hours during the day, during the heaviest sun. Of course, those prone to melanoma need to take extra precaution.

Back to supplements, there are many, such as the fish oils, that are incredibly important for brain function and are especially important for children, to keep them off drugs like Adderall or Ritalin. Get them off these drugs while they're young. Better yet, don't put them on drugs at all. If your way is to take them off somewhere down the road, understand that it will be too late. They'll be addicted, if not physically, then psychologically. I know many parents are wondering what to do about this. Some have even been forced by administrators, as I was, to drug their children or face having them removed from progressive classes. I allowed myself to be bullied at the time, to my eternal regret. I'll tell you about that in the next chapter.

Question everything...

3

A travesty has been perpetrated across the nation, that of the drugging of our children. Almost all American children are on pharmaceuticals, and the rest of the world is following suit. As to why, there are many schools of thought on this, but I'm going to give you one derived from my personal experience.

What is wrong with our school systems? The way children are taught is antithetical to how they actually learn. Not all of our children fit into the learning pattern, and they present a problem in the public school system or even the private schools, who must conform to standardized tests. The students must perform on these tests, or the school will not stay around. Control comes from the top. Teachers have little or no leeway with how and what they teach, and parents and kids have even less.

If the child doesn't fit into the box, if they are independent thinkers, if they are unruly—they will be made to fit in. Why are they unruly? Are they bad kids or are they acting out because they've been given all sorts of toxins in their foods and environments, including the poisons in vaccines? Sugar is a huge offender, as are allergies to things like dairy and wheat. Diary is a toxin. Get it out of your child's diet in all forms. Get out sugar, which includes fruit juice. They may not eat for a few days while you are changing their diet, but they will eat eventually.

Back to Ritalin and Adderall and the ADHD and ADD scam. A scam that now includes psychotropic drugs for schoolchildren, as the medical community is widely adding these and other dangerous hallucinogens to their lists of "treatments." If a child thinks and behaves in a way that is different, and expresses opinions that do not conform to the curriculum, he is going to be ruled a troublemaker and in need of drugs. I experienced this personally. A lot of these children at a very early age sense they are being quashed and fight back in their own way, which is often by being disruptive.

There are other of reasons for disruptive behavior. There could be upsetting things going on in the home. There could be upsetting things happening in the school room. Every parent needs to be aware that there are thinkers and spiritual souls among us, who at very early ages are being deprived an outlet. This applies to all children, but there are some who resist more than others.

These children are put on drugs, and before you know it, they are compromised, conformist, and thinking inside the box, thrown into the rat race like everyone else. Sorry, to be brutal, but it's true. What do you do about it?

First thing is you change the child's diet, fast, and completely. If he is vaccinated, then probably homeopathy is best to counter its effect, and you'll have to consult a classical homeopath for that. When using homeopathy, stick to classical only, for when you start mixing the remedies they become less effective. It's when they lose effectiveness that the medical community has just cause to say it doesn't work. The fact is, only classical homeopathy works. You can challenge me if you want, but I'm going to stick by it, because this has been my experience over the years. I've wasted a lot of time and money with homeopaths who have mixed remedies, while classical does not mix.

How do we address ADD and ADHD? Chiropractic is very important in all stages of our lives, but it's particularly helpful to young children in getting their alignments balanced and neural passages cleared. There are many other forms of helpful therapies, including cranial sacral, and acupuncture. Start with the basics. The basics are a whole healthy diet, with no sugar or diary or white flour. Remove all additives. Eat only unprocessed whole foods. Yes, this is extremely difficult to do, but not impossible.

If you have to starve your child to get them to start eating healthy foods, know that is for their own good, and it is the best thing you will do for them in the long run. Try to eliminate wheat, and especially gluten, which as everyone is now realizing, is incredibly toxic to our bodies. Young children are often allergic to it. Dairy is a huge allergen, but soybeans are genetically modified, so you have to be careful about finding a substitute milk. Same with rice milk and almond milk. Organic coconut milk is a great solution. It tastes great and is very healthy. Finding a milk that works for your family calls for experimentation. When my kids were young I rotated milks. Once, my son caught me pouring soy milk into the regular milk container. "What are you doing? he asked, ever suspicious of my food methods. When he understood what I was doing, he stopped drinking soy milk. So much is psychological with children. You must always be on your toes.

When my kids were very young, I had them on organic goat milk, which was hard to get. It is more expensive, but goat milk is the closest thing to mother's milk in its genetic structure. With no dairy, there are many pitfalls to watch out for and I have stepped into all of them. We have to look for a very, very organic whole product to give them.

Next, get them off medicine of all types. Eliminate stressors like fighting in the home. Don't fight in front of the children or within earshot. If there are other things going on, be aware that your child is incredibly emotionally sensitive, far more than you may realize.

Public schools in particular are notorious for making children who don't fit in the box feel stupid. I've been through it. I know what they do and have seen it happen. They make kids feel deficient in an early grade and it never goes away. Co-educate as much as you possibly can. I am not talking tutors, so they can do better in the school system, I am saying to offer alternate sources of knowledge so they can feel empowered and learn real things. If you can, tutor them at home yourself, so that you know that they are getting their ideas heard. Homeschooling is a wonderful way to go.

Back to school, and the real problem, which is what to do about them passing the test, so that they can get into the better school, so that they can then get into a better college —these are only areas of concerns if you want your whole life regimented and if you want to do what everyone else does. The truth is, life is very different from what you believe it is when you have young children.

Your kids are going to follow their own path no matter what. There is nothing you can do to change who they are. Let me put that a different way. If you have your hopes set on Harvard, let me tell you, Harvard is not what it's cracked up to be. Harvard may be the very worst place for your child, and the same goes for Princeton and other Ivy League schools. I have a relative who is a counselor at one of these institutions. He says that suicidal tendencies are rampant among those who feel they don't fit in. Always look deeper than how things appear on the surface.

Schools are turning out people who are fitting into the system and perpetuating what isn't working in our society. That's all I have to say about that. You have to choose what's best for you and your children, but the point is to rethink the structure that frames your life. The answer might be different from what you think it is. Take a look at what exists outside your mindset by forcing yourself to consider alternatives.

Whatever you do, you should not bend to pressure from school administrators and teachers, as so many including myself have done, and wrongly put your child on drugs in order to ensure "academic success." While their grades may be positively affected, the emotional and physical toll is irrevocable.

Please do accept and apply all that's been said here when it comes to putting young people on drugs of any kind, psychotropics included. Depression and other so-called mental illnesses can arise from any of the aforementioned items, and can be an indication of deep physical toxicity. This toxicity also comes from subliminal programming, particularly from video games. Please do everything possible to keep your child off drugs. I've been there. I've seen both sides. Drugs always have side effects, and more often than not, they worsen the problem.

$$\underline{4}$$

I want to talk about health freedoms. I thought I was going to wait to give politics its own section, but now I realize that it is so interrelated with this topic that they must be discussed together. The fact is, our freedoms as human beings are being taken away one by one. Liberty begins with food and personal health.

When we are forced to vaccinate without a recourse, when we are forced to administer drugs to our children, when children are kidnapped by hospitals who force medical treatment upon them, when we are forced to eat inorganic, artificially produced, non-labeled GMO foodstuffs —because to label it properly would cause people to say, "Whoa, why are you labeling it, is there something wrong with it?" —we are not a free society.

When were are forced into medical insurance programs, with our every financial and medical statistic recorded, when farmers are not allowed to grow their own organic produce and must use Monsanto's artificially produced seeds, when your own organic vegetable garden is declared illegal and forcibly taken down, when your raw milk producer is shut down and criminalized for providing a product that his customers clamor for because pasteurization kills all the good things in your milk —you are not free.

These things and more are occurring across America. Anyone who thinks they are happening for our own good needs to take a closer look.

Examine the people who are creating these rules and regulations. They are not our friends. These are individuals with ties to corporations that are profiting from these endeavors. I can't stress this enough. Don't follow the company line. Look at who is saying what. Look at the truth, and investigate. We are rapidly approaching a non-free society and not just in our health freedoms.

5

Consider this: less than two percent of the earth's population control 99 percent of the world's wealth. What's wrong with this picture? Why are people starving? Why are billionaire tech gurus and media moguls attending secret Bilderburg meetings with politicians?

Consider the fact that the people who have their hands out asking for money to help raise awareness or send food or aid a myriad of other philanthropic efforts, could meet all the world's needs quite easily with a tiny portion of the wealth that is controlled by the two percent. Our rulers, our governors, and our icons are either hypocrites, or pawns, or dupes.

These people, who are asking for money or are telling us that we have to be vaccinated—for instance, Bill Gates whose father happened to be a eugenicist— are doing so for ulterior motive. Just because you like Bill Gates' computers, doesn't mean you should listen to what he says about vaccines. Vaccines do not cure illness. Only a strong immune system cures illness. There is a second set of vaccines available to the rich that do not contain toxins. They have their own biodynamic farms, and underground shelters for when the expected civil or global wars break out.

The only way to confer immunity is through getting sick and fighting it. Vaccines do not confer immunity. Mother's milk boosts immunity. When you don't breastfeed your baby, you're consigning them to weakness right from the start. Never listen to authorities who say it's okay to not breastfeed your baby. In fact, never listen to authorities if you can help it, especially when they say something that doesn't sit right with you.

We left off at personal health and the stressors that create disease, processed foods, lack of sunshine, pharmaceuticals, emotional stress. What's the biggest cause of emotional stress? Fear! Fear is built into the fabric of our society. Fear that our unborn child won't get into the right nursery school unless they register on time. Fear that our children in grammar school will not get into the proper junior high school if we take a family vacation that takes them out of school for a week—a family vacation that might enlighten them far more than any school program.

Fear that if we do not pass the standardized tests schools that teachers are so terrified of the school will lose its funding. Fear that if those children do not pass those tests they are not going to go to a proper college. Of course, if they do not get to the proper college we know for a fact they're not going have a proper job opportunity when they get out.

The truth is, the job that you get out of college is going to put you right back on that track of fear just like the schooling beforehand has done. Do you really want to go inside the corporate structure? If so, why? To make money? What's your true joy in life? That's what you need to follow, not that which is going to be the most lucrative. If you find your true joy in life, you're going to make the best kind of money, and what's more, you'll be giving back to the world.

You also won't die saying, "*What did I do it all for?*" You won't change who you intrinsically are in your path to get there. Because that is what happens. That's the reality of it. I personally saw tons of idealistic NYU grads leave the Stern Business School, stars in their eyes, saying, "I am going to change the world. I am going to help the world." They become Wall Street brokers and bankers and execs just like everyone else. Then they got ground down inside the machinery and changed inside. Are they happy? Probably not.

The most happy people in the world are those who are doing what they want, what they were put on this planet to do. Sometimes this doesn't include making a lot of money. We know money is valuable. We all want it. I am not going to tell you not to get some. But, what then would you do with the money? Buy big boats, big houses, better pottery? Money is important to keep families together and to pay rent and food bills. Clothes are important, as are some electronics, and a car or two. Add in a heat source, gas, and some vacations. Beyond that what would you do with that money? Would you take it and empower the world around you? Like Jesus said, "Give a man a fish and feed him for a day. Give him a fishing pole and feed him for a lifetime." Well, Jesus didn't say that exactly, but it was something like that. I think it had to do with seeds, but you get the picture. If you're going to change the world, how are you going to do that? And, where is your money and effort best spent?

6

This is going to be a short chapter. It's very simple. Despite popular belief, there are no sides to be drawn. Politics are about dividing people and not about representing them. They're about dividing allegiances, diverting attention, drawing us in with new things to worry about, when few of our governors are acting for the people's interest. If they were, there wouldn't be such a thing as campaign contributions. Lobbyists would not be allowed to influence votes. Senators would be forced to settle issues before taking a holiday. No bill could be passed that wasn't easily read and understandable. No addendums would be slipped into said bills and passed without scrutiny. There would be no Federal Reserve. Governors on all levels would take a cut in their huge salaries rather than see the people they represent suffer. There would be an oversight committee enacting punishment for politicians who lie.

And on and on and on.

There is no inherent difference between a democrat and a republican, and likewise, between a conservative and a liberal. These non-humans on TV, these talking heads, these endless talk shows, these endless divisions in the media— are all a diversion. It's meant to divert our attention from the true issue at hand, which is the absolute corruption of our governmental system at the core level. Even honest politicians are turned bad by the system. Coercion and bribery are built into the system leaving them no other way to survive If you speak out, you will be eliminated. A sexual indiscretion usually serves well enough. If not, a larger scandal is created, and the spoil sport is taken down. Witness Kennedy and Lincoln, and many, many others.

As long as we have people representing us with divided interests, they are not our representatives. As long as there is corporate funding of any kind, they are not our governors. They are corporations' governors. When I use the term *governors*, I mean all politicians, officials and monarchs, elected or appointed, or ushered in on the strength of their genetics.

When you appoint people to cabinets in return for different favors, or when you listen to powerful lobbyists, you are no longer a governor. You are beholden to that other interest. So, what's the answer? The answer is, *don't vote.*

I know it's contrary. But the world is upside down. I repeat, don't vote.

Every once in a while, there does seems to be somebody who is telling the truth. In 2012, the lone voice appeared to be Ron Paul. Those people are generally kept under wraps. In Paul's case he was taken out of the race. In Donald Trump's case, he has been bastardized and smeared by the media daily. An illegal campaign was invented before he even came into office citing collusion with foreign parties. The truth is, we need a new way of government. We need governors who are acting for the people. We need to eradicate this current system. The Federal Reserve is not a federal agency but a private one, acting for private interests. It was created as a money-making machine, and the bill was passed in 1913 under the publics' noses on Christmas eve. Like I said, don't believe me. Do your homework.

Lincoln was assassinated for fighting them. Follow the presidents along. Do a search for individual presidents and the Federal Reserve and you'll see they sided with or against them. When they fought them, they were gotten rid of. When they sided with them, they were kept in office.

The individuals who succeeded in getting the Federal Reserve implanted took control of our money system. These are the same people who control the IMF, or the International Monetary Fund, which has succeeded in bringing down country after country by extending credit and then squeezing off that credit. It's a popular tactic.

They did it in Yugoslavia. They did in every country you can think of. Greece, Portugal, Spain and Italy suffered. The fact is nothing is as it seems, including self-imploding countries like Egypt, Syria, and Libya whose rebellions were engineered by the CIA, again, for profit.

There's a very edifying document online called the Illuminati Timeline, that follows, step by step, how the West took down regimes, built them back up, pretended to take them down again, and so on. It's a ploy. We're not creating freedom and democracy if we're warring on other countries. We're killing them for personal gain. We are creating impoverishment and destroying infrastructures so we can put our own brand of colonialism in place. Do you think that we were really looking for weapons of mass destruction in those Iraqi enclaves? No, we were taking down a society.

We are not killing indiscriminately. We are creating war, hatred, and grief with a purpose in mind. The people who are orchestrating this are not humane. They may look like human beings, but they're missing the human component called compassion. Many theories abound about who these individuals are who are running our world and creating war, but let's just say that, despite their many concerned-looking photo ops, they are lacking the qualities that make us human. They care only about power and money.

By way of a hint, you will see that virtually every single person that we've had as a ruler in the United States of America, as well as the European monarchies, is connected by birth if you trace the bloodline back far enough. You as a citizen of this world need to take responsibility for understanding these things. Go ahead and look up the bloodlines. The fact is a small group of people control this planet and have for a very long time.

Now, whether you believe that these are ET's or reptilians or just powermongers gone amuck, is up to you. The various theories out there each have their own level of believability. One thing that is irrefutable is that they use the monetary system to control us and to instill fear. Fear that we're going to not have enough to pay our bills, to pay our interest. Who said money needs to create interest? Who said you need to borrow money to be paid back with interest?

Lincoln didn't, and he wanted to formalize the fiat money system, where money was lent to whoever needed it and was paid it back without interest. Wow! What a revolutionary idea. No interest. Interest which goes, by the way, to the bankers controlling the Federal Reserve, not to American coffers. In fact, every cent of our federal income tax goes to pay the national debt. Who do you think is benefiting from that?

As we keep borrowing, our money is being siphoned off to the bankers, the JP Morgans, the Chases, the Rockefellers and the Rothschilds. It's a very checkable fact. All the information contained herein is checkable. I can't spend the time in giving you every resource to look these things up, but while you still have an internet at your disposal, as well as books and libraries, you should check into all I am telling you. The truth is there for you to find.

Back to money. Eradicate fear of not having enough from your life. I know you have a rent to pay. You have to buy food. You have to grow organic vegetables. The answer is to try to go back to basics as much as you possibly can. A lot of us living in urban areas will find this especially hard, but if we go back to collective growing resources, if we go back to the way our grandparents lived in communities that helped each other, that's the answer. It's hard to do. Maybe it won't happen in our lifetimes, but we can start. I'm not saying to eradicate luxury, I'm not saying not to travel, or not to enjoy the finer things in life, but to discern what's truly valuable and to opt for that instead of the things others tell us are valuable.

This means to stop the high grade consumption. Do you really need that second fried ham? Do you really need two blenders? Do you really need the excess we're used to living with? If you go to other countries in the world, and I don't mean the big hotels that the tourist like to stay in, you'll find others subsist well on far less than we have. They travel more, see friends more, enjoy family more, and work far fewer hours. They also spend far less money buying plastic items from China.

In many places in Europe you'll see a level of excess is missing, except for those who have become Westernized, where the excess has been driven way up. This brings me to the next section... consumers.

7

From the moment we take our very first breath, we are trained to be consumers. I'm talking the Western world here, a Western world that is rapidly taking over the East. Look at India. India is rapidly becoming a consumer society, if not already. Africa is next, if Africa isn't completely destroyed first, that is. How to stop rampant consumerism? Rule number one, turn off the TV.

Yes, I know you love your favorite show. You love this; you love that. Well, you can get virtually every show you have ever dreamed of including your current shows, online for free once you figure it out how to do it. Once you find your TV shows, and begin watching them without commercials, you'll never miss television again.

You will also find that there really aren't that many shows you have to watch. Your list will go down to maybe one or two and even then maybe only one that you have to follow. You'll see that weaning yourself off TV is not as hard as you think.

Second, you need to check and double check each and every purchase that you make. Ask yourself, "Do I really need that?" I am not saying I don't love beautiful clothes. I love beautiful shoes. I mean, I do have too many shoes; I admit it. But, I try to keep my purchases in check and I am trying extremely hard to determine what I do need and what I don't.

Consumerism and commercialism is all around us. Black Friday, Grey Thursday, Cyber Monday, and so on, are just tools used to stupefy us and make us think we need more things, sometimes killing each other in the process. It's a fraud. It is zombifying us and we can say *no* to it.

The third thing is to understand is that we are immersed in a culture of sexualization. Kids are becoming oversexed at younger ages, a certain sign of the destruction of society. This is not bible-thumping mumbo jumbo. This is about taking a good look at what is happening all around us and why. As girls and boys become sexually active at ever younger ages at the cost of their innocence, they also become consumers at increasingly younger ages. The widely publicized debauchery of celebrities and overt gender lies such as boys having periods and sex being undetermined at birth, serve to confuse and oversexualize children at far too young an age. The over-bombardment of our youth with sexual images, is dragging us into a depraved state where we are becoming nothing more than mindless drones who accept everything handed to us. The act of monogamous sex with a loving partner of the opposite sex has all but been eradicated from our society, and the inherent joy and divinity therein, has been reduced to ridicule. This is yet another important argument for homeschooling.

When we've experienced the crumbling values of a moral society, what is left? I know many people feel that if you home school your children they're not going to be socialized properly. Perhaps you think you're not equipped, or that you don't have the time because of your job or career. Again, this is where community comes in, or a supervised tutor while you work from home. If you have the will, you can find the way. There are certainly ways of socializing your child that do not involve being in the school system. If you educate your child within a community you can keep their education close to home at the very least.

If we go back to talking about government for a moment, government should be kept at a level closest to you as possible. The more removed the government is from you personally, the more automated and impersonal it becomes, and the less say you have with your governors. The Southern states may have been on to something and I'm not talking about the ills of slavery, which we all know was an atrocity. I'm talking about states' rights. There is a movement at hand for states to become their own governments and not remain beholden to a federal government, which is widely recognized as not having individual interests at heart.

The indoctrination into the commercial society we live in is all around us, everywhere we look. You have to be aware of it to guard against it. Don't give in to it. Don't say, "Everyone accepts it, so I have to as well." That's no excuse. You can guard against your children seeing inappropriate movies and images by adopting the vigilance that is necessary.

You can monitor them, and when they have experienced something that it is inappropriate for their age range you can explain what it's about. It brings you closer as a parent and it helps them understand what they're not supposed to fall prey to in this very adult world. I'll give you an example. A young girl I know was reading an extremely popular teenage book series, that was made into an even more popular series of movies.

She was eleven, and when her father become aware of the substance of this book, and that the main character gets pregnant by the end, he got very upset and made her stop reading. The young lady was on the last chapter so she became extremely upset herself.

She wanted to find out what happened, but the dad explained how he did not want to see her grow up before her time and how these themes were themes that she was not even familiar with yet, and that they needed to talk about these things before she heard about them somewhere else. When he explained this to her she became calm and understanding.

He allowed her to finish that book, but before she proceeded to the next book in the series, she was to give herself time to grow up a little, a few years, actually. She understood his point and agreed. He understood hers. Kids don't need to grow up as quickly as you think they do. They are relieved when you step in as a parent and say, "This is inappropriate." It's not being a prude. It's just that at the age of ten or eleven or twelve, do girls and boys really need to be thinking about one another in terms of sex? It's too soon.

8

This is going to upset a few people so I'm just going to plunge right in. If you're reading this far, I can assumed that you're at least half interested or half believing in what I'm saying by now. Religion is contrived to divide us and to take away our divinity as individuals. We are meant to be divine. We were created that way. We are supposed to be one with God.

The evils that have been experienced in the name of religion have been the worst evils that have ever been perpetrated on this planet. I'm talking about the Spanish Inquisition, Saint Ptolemy's Day, the Holocaust, which was in part Vatican sponsored, and many, many historical episodes, including the crusades, which have been conducted in the name of religion.

Now, that doesn't mean that Judaism or Islam is better than Christianity or vice versa. Islam advocates the murder of "disbelievers" in the Koran. The Ottoman empire rivaled Rome's in brutal, bloody destruction. Religion by its nature is meant to divide us and to separate individuals from the divine. The divine is something that can be attained on its own. Any of us can find it. All you need to do is tap into your higher self. You do not need to get involved with new age hocus pocus and other woo-woo stuff. All that you desire to attain with God can be achieved on your own.

Let me start again. You do not need priest or a rabbi or anyone else to tell you how to be close to God. You need to do it on your own.

You do not need to be told that you're a sinner. You do not need to be repentant. You do not need to confess your sins to any man or woman. Most priests are fallible in their own right, because they are human like the rest of us. You're repentance is up to you and your God, no one else. Take out the middle man. We don't need excessive government. We don't need our religion, and especially our spirituality, in the hands of someone else.

Would you put the raising of your child into the hands of somebody else? Well, we have in the schools, but would you allow somebody else to completely take over the raising of your child? Don't you want to make your own decisions? Why would you put your divinity or spirituality or family spirituality in the hands of someone who isn't you? Religions are created to divide. Religions were created to quash individual power.

You, me all of us —are infinitely powerful. Now, a church, mosque, or synagogue may make us feel good and give us the sense of community. There's nothing wrong with that. But, when you allow other people to tell you what is divine and what isn't then you are no longer responsible for you divinity and simultaneously you are responsible for all the ills that the church commits in your name.

There is only one way to reach divinity, and that is through faith and unconditional love.

9

You're told when you're young to grow up and marry someone with money, looks and social status. Everybody is pretty much looking for this "perfection" in a mate. Do we really need the person who is the best income provider or the best social status notch? Or, do we need somebody who is completely in touch with him or herself and who is willing to give himself over one hundred percent to becoming a full and faithful, giving partner who holds your relationship sacred?

Have you perceived yet that everything in this world is upside down? You will see that very often our standards and goals are not what they should be. What's called for is a deep examination of your desires and needs to understand that the person who perhaps has the best career or the best prospects is not necessarily the one who's going to give you the love and the connection that you need.

I'm not talking about people who are completely confused or lost in this world. I'm referring to people who have their head on straight. Be aware that the person that is right for you might not be the one that it seems, or you may have passed over the right one, because your goals are not what they should be. What you should be looking for in a mate is the infinite spark, the coming together of two souls who are completely attracted to one another, who will grow together, learn together, and love one another unconditionally. Everything else can be changed through love.

CONCLUSION

It's natural for parents to want to wrap their arms around their children and protect them from all the bad things that might happen in this world, but we know that can't be. Every person needs to be equipped to make his or her own own decisions in the best way possible. I am sure you will learn and make your own choices.

In modern society, we've lost much of our heritage. We've lost contact with our ancestors and the mystery schools known by the original peoples of the earth, who are our true progenitors. Instead, we are in a fast-paced digital world, where we think we have all knowledge at our fingertips. But where is it coming from, and who's bestowing this information?

Information sources always have to be checked and double checked, triple checked and even then, it always comes down to one thing. That's our inner perception and sense of what's right. If something strikes us as not being right, we need to listen to that inner voice. The inner voice is the most reliable guidance that we have.

Listen to this voice and turn knowledge into wisdom, and all will be well.

Unconditional Love to You and Yours Forever,

Lane

Lane Keller is an Author and Reseacher. After being raised in a holistic, spiritual, non-dogmatic household wherein one parent was a mechanical engineer and the other a celebrated psychic, her left and right brains came together in the form of writing that probed the depths of spiritual, physical, humanistic and social truth.

Learn more about Lane at
www.laneexplains.com

www.ingramcontent.com/pod-product-compliance
Lightning Source LLC
Chambersburg PA
CBHW031634040426
42452CB00007B/829